MW00861608

The
Blues Scales
Essential Tools For Jazz Improvisation

by Dan Greenblatt

Editor and Publisher - Chuck Sher
Contributing Editors - Larry Dunlap, David Scott and Jim Rothermel
Music Copying and Editing - Chuck Gee
Cover Graphics - Attila Nagy
Cover Artwork - Kevin Neireiter

Table Of Contents

Acknowledgments

We'd like to thank all the people who were essential to the realization of this project: to Larry Dunlap, Jim Rothermel and David Scott for contributing some cool blues vocabulary; to Michael Zisman and Jim Nadel for help with the text; to Chuck Gee for numerous helpful suggestions and another world-class music copying job; to David Marck, Ed Fuqua and Chris Roselli for their "way deep in the pocket" playing on the accompanying CD; to Peter Karl Studios, Brooklyn, NY for the excellent recording of the CD and Gary Mankin of San Francisco for the masterful mixing and mastering work; to Chuck Stewart, Bill King and Paul Hoeffler for the classic photographs; to Attila Nagy for the cover and text graphics; to Kevin Neireiter (www.jazzlandscapes.com) for the beautiful cover artwork of McCoy Tyner; to all the great jazz musicians past and present who inspire us to learn and grow in the music; and to our families, who made it all possible.

Dan Greenblatt & Chuck Sher

About The Author

Saxophonist and educator Dan Greenblatt spent 24 years on the jazz scene in Seattle, where he was best known for his performances and recordings with bassist/composer Chuck Metcalf and with the Seattle Repertory Jazz Orchestra. In these groups he worked with all of Seattle's top jazz musicians, such as Jay Thomas, Marc Seales, Randy Halberstadt, and Don Lanphere, as well as many national artists including Quincy Jones, Clark Terry, Ernestine Anderson, George Cables, Arturo Sandoval, Jimmy Heath, and Frank Wess. As an educator, Dan was the saxophone and improvisation coach for ten years for Seattle's award-winning and nationally recognized jazz programs at Washington Middle School, Garfield High School and Roosevelt High School.

Greenblatt moved to New York in 2002 to teach at LaGuardia High School for the Performing Arts. He joined the faculty of the Jazz & Contemporary Music Program at New School University in 2003, and became the program's Director of Academic Affairs in 2004.

INTRODUCTION • Starting With The Blues Scales

BEGINNERS

Even if all you know is the basics of how to play your chosen instrument (how to read the notes on the staff, the major and minor scales, some chord arpeggios, how to count beats in a measure, etc.), you are ready to use this book to begin learning how to play jazz.

In this book we will show you how to create meaningful jazz solos, even if your technical proficiency and knowledge of music theory are limited, using the Blues Scales (yes, there are more than one!). You will learn to acquire and employ a blues vocabulary so that your playing will start to sound like real music quickly, rather than at some distant point in the future.

Besides its practical value, we chose this approach because it mirrors the development of jazz itself, which was rooted in the blues and basic tonal centers—rather than elaborate chord changes—until the advent of bebop in the 1940s. We'll be looking at examples of phrases by swing masters Lester Young, "Sweets" Edison, and Johnny Hodges; boppers including Charlie Parker and Dizzy Gillespie; modern improvisers and composers including Dexter Gordon, Horace Silver, Cannonball Adderley, and Miles Davis; funk and fusion players such as Michael Brecker, David Sanborn, and Jaco Pastorius; and many others. From these great artists you will learn how to use this most basic vocabulary of the jazz language.

Please follow all the instructions given so that you take the process outlined here step-by-step. The results will be well worth the effort you expend. And don't forget to Have Fun!

Useful Background Information

In case you haven't learned these yet, we include here the three most basic types of chords used in jazz—major seventh, dominant seventh and minor seventh—and the scales most commonly played with them. (There are other scales that fit these chords as well, but these are the most basic ones.) You will, of course, eventually need to know these basic scales and chords in all 12 keys.

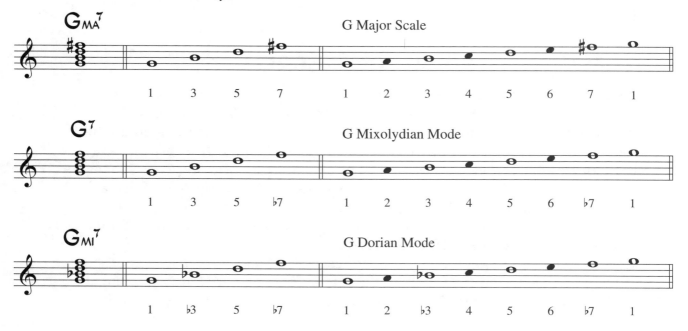

Underneath each note on the previous page is a number called the "scale degree", which reflects that note's position in the scale when counting up from the first, or "root", note of the scale. We will be using the concept of scale degrees often in this book.

Later we will also be using Roman numerals when analyzing the relationships of chords to a tonal center. These Roman numerals refer to the scale degree which is the root from which a chord is built. We use uppercase Roman numerals for chords that have a major 3rd in them, and lowercase ones to indicate chords with a minor, or flatted, 3rd.

For example, for a song in the key of G, a chord built on the note G that contained a major 3rd (the note B), would be notated as the "I-chord." The chord built on the 5th degree of the G major scale (the note D) would be called a "V-chord", since it too usually has a major 3rd. The chord built on the third degree of the G major scale (the note B) usually has a minor 3rd, so it would be notated as the "iii-chord."

MORE ADVANCED PLAYERS

Even if you use the Blues Scales regularly in your own playing, we are sure that you will benefit by going through the exercises in this book, especially from Chapter 3 onward. But first, please play along with the CD tracks for Chapters 1 and 2 and have fun with our swinging, state-of-the-art New York rhythm section! Please also make sure that you understand all the concepts—especially the importance of the Major Blues Scale—before proceeding.

Photo©Chuck Stewart

**MILES DAVIS
(with Cannonball Adderley & Jimmy Cobb)**

CHAPTER 1 • Basic Blues Theory

If you want to learn how to play jazz, one of the best places to begin is with the blues. There are several reasons for this.

First of all, the basic Blues form is one of the simplest in all of jazz.

Second, the basic Blues form is extremely widespread. There are hundreds of commonly played jazz pieces based on the Blues structure, and it also is central to most other forms of contemporary music. So when you learn how to improvise on the Blues, you are dealing with something familiar and you learn something that will be of continuing value.

Finally, the basic Blues form is extremely flexible, with many variations, and it is a form to which you will return throughout your development as an improviser. Rather than leaving the Blues behind as you get more sophisticated, you bring the Blues along with you on your path of development.

Getting Started

EXERCISE #1

Let's start with a fairly simple Blues at a relaxed tempo, the "First Step Blues." Read through the melody a few times at a comfortable tempo. Then listen carefully to how the melody is played on the saxophone track (CD Track #1 , first two choruses).

Finally, try to play the melody along with the rhythm section by turning off the saxophone track on the left channel. Try imitating the swing feel and the quarter-note articulation from the saxophone track.

CD Track #19 has both Bb and A tuning notes, if you need them.

In the Bb and Eb versions of the book, all notes and chords have been transposed into your key.

First Step Blues
Dan Greenblatt

After the melody, the rhythm section continues to play the Blues form for several choruses, and then the saxophone comes back in with the melody at the end. That middle section, with the rhythm section playing the Blues form, is your chance to do some improvising. But the big question is, "What notes should I use to improvise with?" The most common answer is "use the Blues Scale" in the key of the tune. In the key of G, it looks like this:

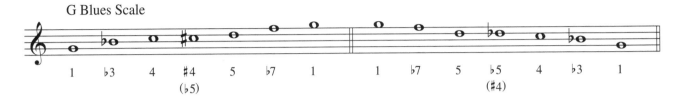

The "Blues Scale" provides the beginning improviser with several things of value. For one, it greatly simplifies the problem of playing on the chord changes. You simply stay on the same scale throughout your solo, and ignore the changes. Moreover, the "Blues Scale" has a familiar, "down-home" sound, so you can capture a "blue" mood almost without effort.

Problems with the "Blues Scale"

There is a major problem with this typical advice, however, which is that aspiring improvisers using this approach almost always sound bad. There are two main reasons for this.

First of all, the "Blues Scale" is missing too many important notes. This makes it a very limited vehicle, unable to carry the variety of phrases and moods that allow you to create contrasts and develop a story-like improvisation. The biggest missing note in this scale is the major 3rd, and also missing are the 2nd and 6th notes of the major scale. So the common six-note "Blues Scale" effectively handcuffs you, paints you into a corner. The effort to simplify ends up oversimplifying.

The second reason that "Blues Scale" solos generally sound bad is that they contain no motion, no harmonic movement. Almost all jazz involves "playing the changes," where your improvisation reflects the harmonic motion of the song. Exclusive use of the "Blues Scale" provides a fundamentally static approach to a fundamentally dynamic art form.

The vast majority of beginning improvisers, however, are not ready to absorb the complex system of chords and scales that evolved jazz musicians use. So the puzzle becomes one of developing an approach that is simple, but not too simple, which retains the advantages of the "Blues Scale" without missing the other good notes, and which gets you playing changes without requiring you to digest the entire system of Western Harmony.

There are Two "Blues Scales!"

The solution to the puzzle is that there are really **two** basic Blues Scales that are commonly used by jazz improvisers, rather than one single scale. One is the Blues Scale we already looked at. Because of its b3rd, this scale has a decidedly minor sound, so from now on we will refer to it as the "Minor Blues Scale."

G Minor Blues Scale

The second Blues Scale has a decidedly major sound because of the inclusion of the major 3rd (even though it also contains the minor 3rd as well). We will call this scale the "Major Blues Scale." In the key of G, it looks like this:

G Major Blues Scale

Practicing the Scales

EXERCISE #2

First you need to thoroughly learn and memorize the notes in these two scales, including the whole range from the lowest to the highest notes you can play on your instrument. As one method of really learning the scales inside-and-out, we encourage you to compose scalar exercises that both rehearse the scale notes and simultaneously have a satisfying melodic contour. For example, try this one-and-a-half octave version of the G Major Blues Scale:

EXERCISE #3

Here is a sample way to practice the G Minor Blues Scale, again with a line that has some melodic interest:

EXERCISE #4

Here are more examples of both Blues Scales for you to learn:

EXERCISE #5

After you are comfortable playing these examples, use the blank staves below to write some G Blues Scale melodies out, both Major and Minor. Again, play these through enough so that you are comfortable with them, so that you "own" them.

Practicing Movement Between Scales

EXERCISE #6

Now that you have broken out of the shackles of the single Blues Scale, you need to learn how to move back and forth between the two scales at particular times, as the harmony of the blues changes. This can be a huge step for many, so it might take a while for you to get the hang of it. You can start by practicing moving back and forth between the two scales every four bars.

a) One way to do this is simply to combine some of the lines you have already learned in Exercises #2-4 into single eight-bar exercises. For example:

(continued on following page)

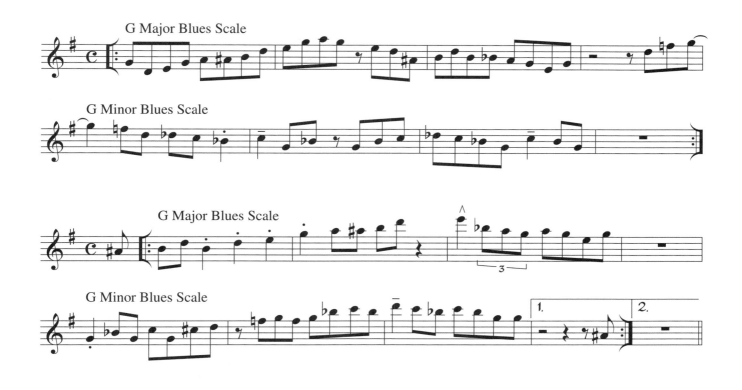

b) Another way to practice moving between the two scales is to start with a Major Blues Scale phrase and then adapt it to the Minor Blues Scale, keeping the same melodic contour. For example, the first four bar phrase in this exercise:

EXERCISE #7

Playing the previous exercise begins to prepare your ear and fingers for changing back and forth between two Blues Scales in the same key. But since improvisation is not done by reading music, this exercise is only of value for your improvisation if it is played from *memory*. You have to get used to hearing rather than seeing what comes next!

CD Track #2 will help you to practice this skill. Turn off the saxophone channel, so that you hear only the rhythm section, and play along with them using the chord chart below. When the rhythm section is on the I-chord (G7) for the first four bars, play G Major Blues Scale phrases you have *memorized* from Exercises #2, #4 and #5. Then when the rhythm section moves to the IV-chord (C7), play G Minor Blues Scale phrases you have *memorized* from Exercises #3, #4 and #5.

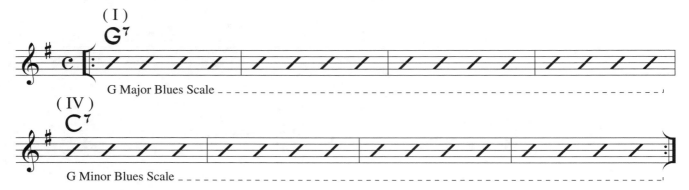

Theory Review - In the above chord progression, the G7 is called the "I-chord" since it is built on the first degree of the G Mixolydian Mode (a "bluesy" version of the G Major scale, with a flatted 7th degree.) The I-chord is also referred to as the "tonic" chord. The C7 is built on the 4th degree of the scale, so it is referred to as the "IV-chord." It is always helpful to think of the scale degree when looking at the chords in a tune.

EXERCISE #8

While it is good to practice memorizing phrases and then playing them at the appropriate time, people do not usually play long memorized phrases verbatim when they are actually improvising.

An important skill that *will* really help you begin to improvise is learning how to take shorter phrases and *develop* them during the time period that the chord remains the same. These shorter phrases may be fragments of longer phrases that you have already learned.

Now return to CD Track #2 and listen to it with the saxophone track turned on. On the next page, we have transcribed the first part of what the saxophone plays for you to study. Notice the use of repetition, both of notes and rhythms. Sometimes only part of the phrase is repeated, so that the idea *develops* instead of merely being restated.

EXERCISE #9

Now you are ready to try making up your own melodies, alternating scales every four bars. Turn off the saxophone channel on CD Track #2 and try playing along with it using the following suggestions:

1) The melodies do not have to be long lines of 8th notes.

2) They can involve repetition of the same phrase (or part of a phrase) one or more times within the four bars.

3) They don't have to start on the roots of the scales.

4) They don't have to use the scale notes in scale order.

5) They almost certainly should make use of rests.

After four bars of melodies from one scale, switch to the other scale and make melodies for the next four bars. Then return to the first scale. Now you are improvising on the two scales, and making the change between the scales on time.

11

(For people having trouble with Exercise #9)

Some readers may find it difficult to improvise on changing scales. Melodies just don't pop into your mind rapidly enough to fill up the four bars. Or else you are so busy thinking about what to play and trying to play it that you lose track of the form and change scales at the wrong time. If so, try the following intermediate steps (Exercises #10 through #13):

EXERCISE #10

In the blank staves below, compose at least two more four-bar sections yourself, using each scale. Take your time and make sure that you have four-bar phrases that you feel comfortable with. After they are written down, please memorize each phrase so that you don't have to read it anymore.

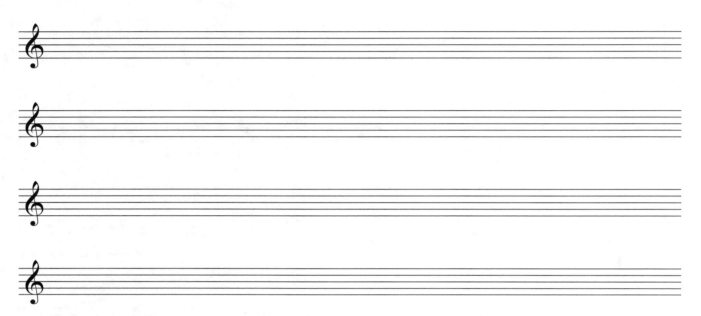

EXERCISE #11

Make sure that you have thoroughly memorized at least four Major and four Minor Blues phrases, choosing from among the ones that appear in Exercises #4, #6, #8 and the ones you wrote yourself in Exercise #10. Now, playing along with CD Track #2, see if you can alternate between the two scales in four-bar chunks—but instead of spontaneously composing melodies you will be plugging in the pre-composed melodies. This is a form of improvising, since some of the phrases are ones you invented, and you are also making the choices as to which melody gets played when. *The idea is to hear the phrase clearly in advance, know exactly where it belongs, and then play it at the right time.*

EXERCISE #12

Once you get the hang of popping various memorized phrases into the correct four-bar slots, you should try to increase the level of spontaneity. You don't have to jump straight into complete freedom—try altering one of your memorized phrases on the fly, or using only half of the memorized phrase, and then trying to develop that part of the phrase in the next two bars before you switch scales.

EXERCISE #13

If you are still having trouble learning how to switch from one scale to another, use simpler melodic ideas, ones having more rests in them, so that you will have more time to hear and execute the new scale at the correct time.

Different Rates of Movement

In order to handle the blues progression, you will need to be able to switch scales at varying rates of speed. Sometimes you will stay with one scale for two bars, sometimes for only one bar. So now you need to practice switching scales with different rates of movement.

EXERCISE #14

This example goes back and forth between the two scales every two bars. **CD Track #3** will give you an accompaniment to practice this concept with, as well as a model for how it's done on the saxophone channel.

EXERCISE #15

This exercise moves back and forth between the two Blues Scales every measure.
CD Track #4 will give you an accompaniment to practice this concept with, as well as a
model for how it's done on the saxophone channel. We've transcribed what the saxophone
plays on this track for you to study, and then just the rhythm section continues for you to
play along with.

The skill of juggling two different sources of melodic material is by no means an easy one
for many beginning musicians to master, so don't be discouraged. Use Exercises #10-13 if
you get stuck, and continue to simplify your melodic ideas until you find something that you
can execute comfortably while switching back and forth each bar.

EXERCISE #16

Now, in the staves below, compose your own exercises switching scales every bar, and practice them along with CD Track #4 until they are memorized and comfortable to play.

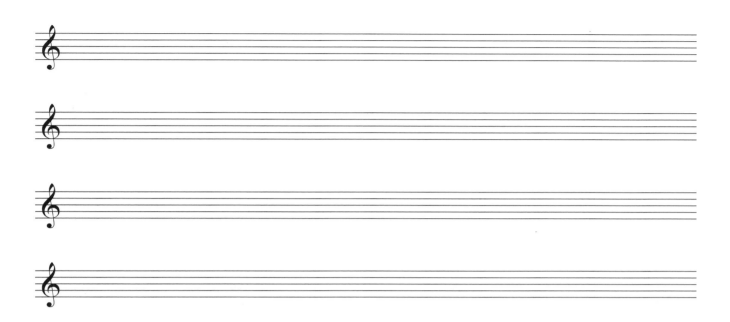

Caveat (A Fancy Latin Word for "Warning")

Before moving on to consider how to apply these ideas to improvising on the blues, please note that this concept of two Blues Scales is still a simplification. A great deal of real blues improvising in the jazz style still does not fit into either of these two scales. But our system does succeed in giving you access to all of the "real" notes that jazz improvisers use when playing the blues.

Later in the book we will see how to extend these two basic scales to make them even more useful. So while this system is a simplification, it is not (like the single Blues Scale approach) an oversimplification. Rather it is inclusive enough to provide the kind of broad and flexible foundation needed for soloing that you (as a developing jazz improviser) really can use.

15

Using the Two Blues Scales

Let's look at a classic jazz-style blues, "Sandu" by the great Clifford Brown. We have put it in the key of G to make it easier to see its relationship with the two Blues Scales explained already. And we have simplified the chord changes to a very basic form of the blues.

©1962 (Renewed 1990) Second Floor Music (BMI). All Rights Reserved Including Public Performance For Profit. Used by Permission.

Look at the opening phrase of "Sandu." The notes used are 1, b3, 3, 5, 6, 5 and 8 (1) of the key of the piece, making it a typical Major Blues Scale lick. Only the notes of the Major Blues Scale are used (with one exception) through the third bar, although the notes in bar 2 could be either scale.

If you analyze the notes in bars 5 and 6 (and the pick-up notes to that phrase found at the end of bar 4), you'll see that they fit the G Minor Blues Scale. In bar 7, when the chord shifts back to the I-chord (also known as the tonic), the major 3rd reappears. In bars 9 and 10, where the blues progression moves to the V-chord, the Minor Blues Scale is used. In bar 11 the Major Blues Scale is again used on the tonic chord.

This analysis of "Sandu" is incomplete and leaves out several notes, but a couple of things are clear:

First, the melody moves back and forth between the Major and Minor Blues Scales.

Second, this movement is timed to correspond with the basic chord movement. In particular, it seems that on the I-chord, Brownie's melody is based on the Major Blues Scale; elsewhere, the Minor Blues Scale predominates. Thus, we have discovered an important generalization:

The First Principle for Blues Improvisation

On the I-chord, use phrases derived from the **Major Blues Scale**;
On the IV- and V-chords, use phrases derived from the **Minor Blues Scale**.

Let's go back to the most basic blues progression and use the "First Principle" to create the appropriate blues scales (G Major Blues Scale or G Minor Blues Scale), which you will see listed underneath each bar. The chords and scales will look like this:

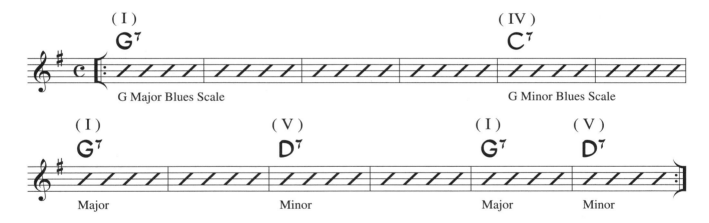

17

EXERCISE #17

Along with **CD Track #5** try playing the first three choruses of what the saxophone plays, transcribed below. After listening to the sample solo the saxophone plays on this track, turn the saxophone channel off, try playing what is written here and then use the rest of this track to come up with your own variations on the ideas you have learned so far. Be sure to follow the timing of the scale changes as exactly as you can to match the scales listed underneath each bar.

(continued on following page)

Photo©Bill King, Toronto, ON **JOHN SCOFIELD**

EXERCISE #18

Here is a little more complex chord progression on the blues that is more like what a typical jazz group would use.

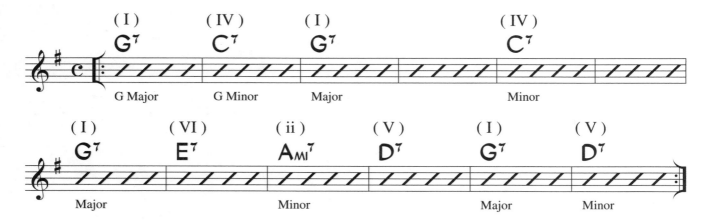

The transcribed solo on these changes seen below is a bit more complex as well. Please notice, however, that the two Blues Scales are still the only scales used and that they change at the same points as Exercise #17 (except for an extra scale change in bar 2). The chords on this exercise give us *a more comprehensive "First Principle for Blues Improvisation."*

> On the I-chord, iii-chord or VI-chord, use phrases based on the **Major Blues Scale**.
> Everywhere else, use phrases based on the **Minor Blues Scale**.

Play the following solo on this blues, note for note, along with **CD Track #6**. After the written material is done, the rhythm section keeps playing so you can make up your own variations on it, changing as little or as much of it as you want. Be sure to follow the timing of the scale changes as exactly as you can to match the scales listed underneath each bar.

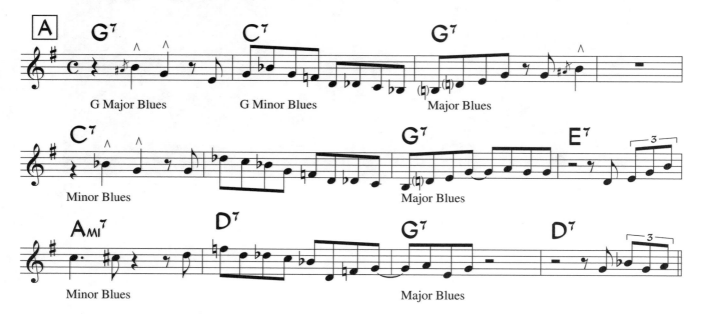

(continued on following page)

Anyone who knows jazz (or classical) harmony might notice a problem with the approach we have been using—i.e., there is an imperfect correspondence between the notes of the Blues Scales and some of the notes in the chord changes.

We understand these contradictions but ask for your forbearance for two important reasons. First, we are trying to simplify things here so that beginning improvisers can get involved in playing the blues and in changing scales without having to confront the entire system of jazz theory. And second, good sounding solos can be made using only our First Principle; and that, of course, is the most important goal of teacher and student alike.

Vocabulary

Many beginning improvisers never get beyond musical gibberish because they do not learn and play meaningful jazz vocabulary when they improvise. They play notes, but not phrases. And, just as we do with spoken language, we get meaning from phrases and sentences, not individual words strung together.

So you need to learn vocabulary, not just scales. You do need to understand what scale the vocabulary belongs to, so that you know when it is appropriate to use the phrase. But knowing the scales in themselves without knowing any vocabulary really gets you almost nowhere. Wandering aimlessly on the right scale is not a lot better than wandering aimlessly on the wrong scale—only less patently offensive.

On the other hand, even inappropriate phrases engage the knowledgeable listener in a significant way. Moreover, once you have played a clear idea, you can be guided into a better sense of how to use the idea. Your teacher or peers can say to you, "I dig what you're trying to say here, but it doesn't really fit the chord you were using it on. Try altering it like this..."

Your goal is not simply to play along with the music as it goes by. The goal is to say what you think and feel as you are playing, and you need phrases to say what you think and feel.

So, on pages 23-29, we have compiled a collection of classic blues phrases whose notes belong to the Major or Minor Blues Scales. It will take a while to digest all the phrases here, and this section will be one that you might want to come back to periodically to get more inspiration from.

Even more important, however, you must continue to learn phrases that you make up yourself or hear others play if you want to progress. We strongly urge you to keep a notebook of phrases that you've discovered while practicing, phrases you transcribe from recordings, phrases that your teacher or friends show you, etc. This is a lifelong process that will only deepen as time goes on.

All of the phrases in this collection are, moreover, flexible. You do not have to play them in exactly the form in which they appear on the following pages. For example, the opening phrases of "Sandu," Charlie Parker's "Parker's Mood" and Horace Silver's "Sister Sadie" are really the same idea, derived from the Major Blues Scale, realized in three different ways.

a) from "Sandu" by Clifford Brown

b) from "Parker's Mood" by Charlie Parker

c) from "Sister Sadie" by Horace Silver

Answering the "Cliche" Objection

One common objection to a vocabulary-based approach is that you wind up learning old, hackneyed licks rather than developing your own personal and original way of expressing yourself. However, there are three reasons why we feel that this phrase-based approach is crucial at the beginning stages of learning to play jazz.

First, people learn a language by learning the common vocabulary in that language. If you set out to learn Spanish but restrict yourself only to those phrases which you have made up yourself, you won't be able to get far when you go to Mexico.

Second, using familiar phrases is not necessarily a barrier to developing your own original manner of musical expression. Some great artists do invent their own vocabulary, but many are successful by using existing vocabulary in fresh, imaginative, and personally distinctive ways. Dexter Gordon, for example, is widely admired as one of the great artists of the tenor saxophone, yet his actual vocabulary is far from original. So, as you learn the material on the following pages, please remember that these familiar-sounding blues phrases can and should be "personalized" by creating your own variations of them.

Finally, there is a practical issue. There are undoubtedly a few musicians out there who will develop highly original vocabularies. Those rare individuals all have extremely active musical imaginations that are constantly searching for and generating new ideas. Such imaginative musicians generally tend to learn the language on their own. This book is addressed to the rest of us mere mortals who need some help. And the best advice we can offer is: *Build a vocabulary for yourself of familiar-sounding phrases based on each Blues Scale, instead of just running up and down the scales themselves! You can work on originality later.*

Major Blues Phrases (in G)

(Major Blues Phrases - continued)

Photo©Paul Hoeffler, Toronto, ON

DIZZY GILLESPIE

Minor Blues Phrases (in G)

(continued on following page)

29

(Minor Blues Phrases - continued)

EXERCISE #19

Let's take one Major Blues phrase and one Minor Blues phrase and see how you might tackle practicing them so that they become a part of your working vocabulary.

Below is a transcription of what the saxophone plays on **CD Track #7**. First, watch the music go by, then try to play it along with the saxophone. Finally, turn off the saxophone channel and try using the G Major Blues phrase in bar 1 and the G Minor Blues phrase in bar 2 as demonstrated here—i.e., playing them, and variations on them, whenever the appropriate scale comes up. Do this until they really feel like they are "yours." We know that a real-life solo would not use this much repetition, but as a practice technique, we think you will find it invaluable. If so, try it on other phrases too.

CHAPTER 2 • Changing Keys: Transposition

Everything you did in Chapter 1 was in a single key, concert Bb. But if you want to play jazz with other musicians, you will find that you need to play the blues in more than one key. Ultimately you will need to be able to play in all twelve keys, but the vast majority of blues tunes in the jazz style are played in just five of the twelve keys—E, D, A and C, as well as G. (These are transposed to Eb, not concert keys.)

Instead of learning a separate vocabulary for each key, you will learn in this chapter how to transpose what you already know into other keys. The essential skill involved is to think of each phrase not in terms of the names of the notes used, but instead in terms of the relationship of those notes to the key. Let's start with a simple blues idea that derives from the Minor Blues Scale—a piece of Miles Davis' tune "Pfrancin':"

After you have learned this phrase in G by memorizing the names of the notes, you must also think of the notes as scale degrees of G, and those scale degrees can then be transferred to any other key. Below is the same phrase transposed to the key of D with the scale degrees of each note given underneath it.

In the staves provided below, transpose this phrase into the keys of A (first line) and E (second line). Then play the phrase in each of the four keys to make sure you have done the transposition correctly. Your ear will tell you if you have it right.

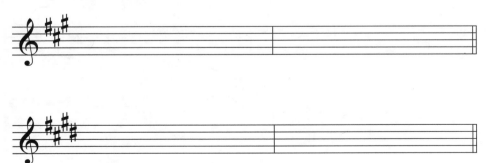

You probably will have discovered by now that your ability to transpose quickly and accurately depends on how well you know the relevant scale in the key to which you are transposing—the "target key." If you are shaky on your E Minor Blues Scale, for example, you may stumble in your effort to find the right notes.

This means that you will need to practice the Major and Minor Blues Scales in the common keys until you know without hesitation what notes belong to each scale, and you are thoroughly comfortable with the fingerings (or positions) involved.

The best way to do this is to return to Exercises #2 and #3 in Chapter 1. Start with the line in Exercise #2, which outlines the Major Blues Scale, and analyze the notes from the point of view of their relationship to the key of G.

Now play the line through several times, slowly, from memory, listening carefully to the sound of the line. As you go through the line, don't think of the names of the notes. Instead, think of their scale degree **numbers** so that you will thoroughly understand their relationship to the key center.

Once you can play it in the familiar key with a comfortable understanding of the scale numbers, you should try, very slowly, to play the same line starting on D. Don't write the notes down in the key of D—do the transposition in your head.

Remember that what you are trying to learn here is how to improvise, and improvisers usually do not have the luxury of being able to write down what they want to play ahead of time. Improvisers play the music that is in their heads, not what is in front of their eyes. If you stop to write it down, you deprive yourself of an opportunity to learn how to use the relationships between the notes spontaneously, while you are playing your instrument.

EXERCISE #20

At the beginning of the next chapter, we move the key center of the blues from G to D. In order to be able to play along with the rhythm section, you will need to know, and be able to play comfortably, the Major and Minor Blues Scales in the key of D.

So, you should go through the same process in D that you did in G, i.e., in the key of D, play through the same Exercises in Chapter 1 that you used to learn the G Blues Scales. You will probably find it easier to do this in a second key now that the ideas are already embedded in you in the previous key.

EXERCISE #21

In the same way that you learned how to switch back and forth between the G Major and Minor Blues Scales at various rates (four bars, two bars, one bar), you need to learn the same skill in the key of D.

To help you we have provided **CD Tracks #8, #9 and #10**. These are essentially the same as CD Tracks #2, #3, and #4, except that we have changed the key from G to D. The author plays the same musical ideas at the beginning of each track, which you will find written out on the next two pages.

33

a) CD Track #8

b) CD Track #9

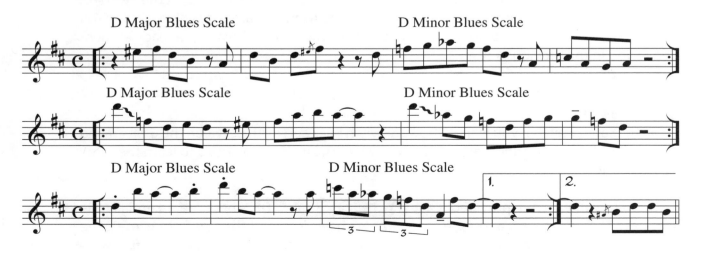

(continued on following page)

34

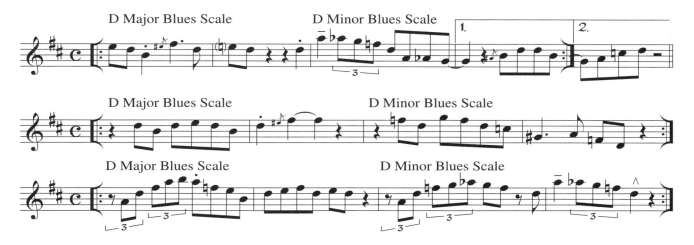

c) **CD Track #10**

EXERCISE #22

Then, finally, you need to learn some vocabulary, some useful musical phrases, that derive from these scales, so that you can improvise as meaningfully in the key of D as you did in G.

CD Track #11 is a medium tempo blues in D, combining the ideas presented in CD Tracks #5 and #6. It starts with the simpler of the two progressions you played on in Chapter 1, and then changes to the more complicated one in the middle of the piece.

Please use this track to practice transposing blues scale phrases you learned in Chapter 1 into the key of D. At the end of the CD (CD Tracks #16, 17 and 18) you will find blues in the keys of A, E and C that you can use to practice this same skill of transposing to the other common keys.

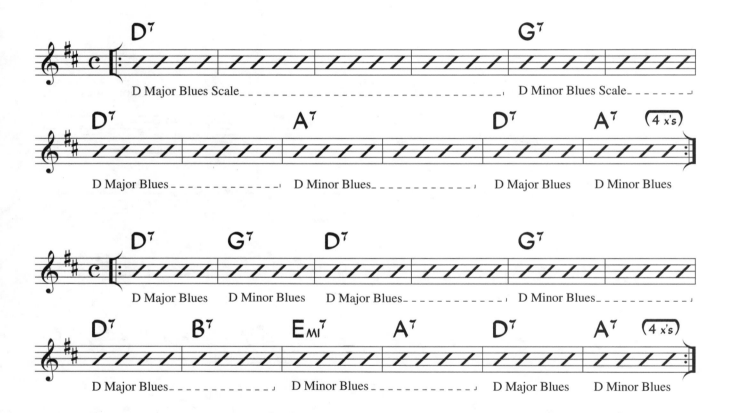

Finally, please note that each Major Blues Scale contains the same notes as the Minor Blues Scale starting down a minor 3rd. For example, the G Major Blues Scale consists of the same notes as the E Minor Blues Scale. The only difference (and it is a big difference!) is what is heard as the tonic note.

This is the same as the relationship between major and their relative minor keys, by the way; e.g., the D major scale has the same notes as the B natural minor scale.

For reference, here are the correspondences between the 12 sets of Major and Minor Blues Scales:

Bb Major Blues Scale has the same notes as the G Minor Blues Scale
Eb Major Blues Scale has the same notes as the C Minor Blues Scale
Ab Major Blues Scale has the same notes as the F Minor Blues Scale

Db Major Blues Scale has the same notes as the Bb Minor Blues Scale
Gb Major Blues Scale has the same notes as the Eb Minor Blues Scale

B Major Blues Scale has the same notes as the G# Minor Blues Scale
E Major Blues Scale has the same notes as the C# Minor Blues Scale
A Major Blues Scale has the same notes as the F# Minor Blues Scale

D Major Blues Scale has the same notes as the B Minor Blues Scale
G Major Blues Scale has the same notes as the E Minor Blues Scale
C Major Blues Scale has the same notes as the A Minor Blues Scale
F Major Blues Scale has the same notes as the D Minor Blues Scale

Photo©Paul Hoeffler, Toronto, ON

**JOHNNY HODGES
(with Aaron Bell)**

CHAPTER 3 • Stretching The Rules

A New Set of Shackles

Once you begin to get the hang of the basic rules for blues improvisation and can switch back and forth between phrases from the two Blues Scales at appropriate times, you will probably find yourself boxed in by the rigidity of the two-scale system. You will have traded in the one-blues-scale shackles for a new and less restrictive two-blues-scale set.

While we contend that a lot of very fine music can be improvised while staying strictly within the constraints of the two-scale system, we recognize that the system is limiting, artificial, and in need of more flexibility. So, this chapter will give you some suggestions for how you can bend, stretch, and ultimately break the basic rules, while still staying faithful to the blues, and the jazz tradition.

EXERCISE #23

Please read through the following three-chorus solo based on the blues, which shows how you can stretch the basic Blues Scales rules presented in Chapter 1. Please watch the music go by first and then try to play it yourself along with **CD Track #12**. There are extra choruses of just rhythm section for you to practice making up your own variations.

This example still uses some phrases that fall strictly within one Blues Scale or the other, and the basic movement between scales follows the First Principle of Blues Improvisation (Major Blues on I, iii, VI; Minor Blues elsewhere). But there are a number of differences as well which we will look at as this chapter progresses.

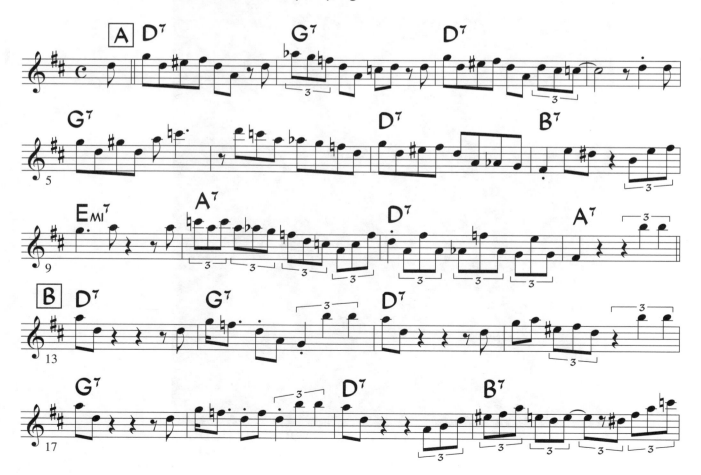

38

(Exercise #23 continued)

Adding Notes to the Blues Scales

One direction you can go in to break the Blues Scale shackles is to begin adding notes to each of the scales. For example:

1) Adding the 4th to the Major Blues Scale (from Oscar Pettiford's "Blues In The Closet")

2) Adding the flatted 7th to the Major Blues Scale (from Charlie Parker's "Bluebird")

3) Adding the 6th or the 9th to the Minor Blues Scale

4) Adding chromatic notes used to connect scale notes in either Blues Scale (from Thelonious Monk's "Blue Monk")

These additions will open up new possibilities for the discovery and creation of blues vocabulary. They will allow you to sound much less mechanical, since the added notes usually come from the other scale, thus making the distinction between the two scales more subtle.

The first chorus of Exercise #23 contains several examples of how this approach can bear fruit. The basic motif, used in bars 1, 3 and 7, is a Major Blues idea, but with the 4th degree of the scale added. In bar 4, the b7th is added to the Major Blues Scale, while in bar 7, the scale is "chromaticized" to fill in the notes between the 5th and the major 3rd. Please go through Exercise #23 again and look for these added notes.

The overall result of these added notes is to provide a richer vocabulary and to make the sound of the switches between the two scales much less predictable and obvious.

EXERCISE #24

What follows are more examples of these extended, hybrid versions of the Blues Scales. Please read through them all first, if you want, but then go back and take one at a time and play along with any of the CD tracks until the phrase is thoroughly incorporated into your own playing. Feel free to play variations of the phrase, use only part of the phrase as a motif to play around with, etc. Please also practice transposing these phrases into other keys, a crucial skill.

More phrases which use the Major Blues Scale with the 4th added:

Here are some blank staves for you to write down your own phrases using this idea:

More phrases which use the Major Blues Scale with the b7th added:

(continued on following page)

Here are some blank staves for you to write down your own phrases using this idea:

43

Phrases that add both the 4th and the b7th to the Major Blues Scale:

Here are some blank staves for you to write down your own phrases using this idea:

Phrases using a chromaticized version of the Major Blues Scale:

Phrases using a chromaticized version of the Minor Blues Scale:

Phrases that add either the 6th or the 9th to the Minor Blues Scale:

Using the "Wrong" Scale

We obviously do not advocate using the Minor Blues Scale all the time (that's where we began the book), but we don't deny that it can be effectively used on the I-chord, if it is used judiciously. For example, Charlie Parker starts off his last chorus of one version of "Now's The Time" with a Minor Blues phrase, after earlier choruses were all based on Major.

Here is an example of Clifford Brown doing the same thing on "Blues Walk."

Similarly, the Major Blues Scale can be used effectively on the V7 chord from time to time. Exercise #23 contains one such instance, in the third chorus, bars 33-34.

It is also possible to stay with the Major Blues Scale on the IV-chord. But take care to avoid landing hard on the major third of the scale (B) in those instances, since that will clash badly with the b7th of the chord (Bb) a half step away. A classic example of this technique is found in Sonny Rollins'"Tenor Madness:"

It is also possible—and indeed quite common—to use both scales more or less at once. For example, here is Cannonball Adderley playing on the tune "Wabash" and going from the Minor Blues Scale to the Major in one phrase:

Here's another example of Cannonball's melding both scales, this time from "Work Song."

EXERCISE #25

Either on your own, or along with any of the CD tracks enclosed, try using this approach yourself of mixing the two blues scales in a single line. There are endless possibilities here. We've included a few blank staves here for you to write down any inspirations you might have.

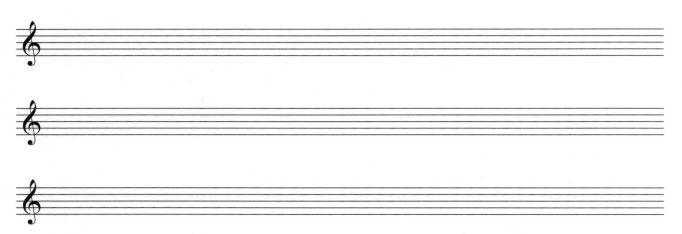

Playing Chord Tones

A third direction in which you can steer in order to loosen up the rules is to make use of tones that come from the chord changes instead of the two Blues Scales. This is especially effective in bar 8 of the blues, where many modern versions include a VI7 chord, leading to the ii7-V7-I sequence commonly used in bars 9-11. The third of the VI7 chord provides you with an eloquent note (D#, if we are in the key of D) that is in neither of the Blues Scales. Exercise #23 repeatedly uses this chord tone.

EXERCISE #26

Please go back and play along with CD Track #6 and try inserting this note on bar 8 each chorus. Here are two examples of this idea, as recorded by a) Charlie Parker and b) Sonny Rollins.

(continued on following page)

Moving an Idea Between I and IV

After you understand how to introduce chord tones into an improvisation which is fundamentally based on Blues Scale vocabulary, you are ready to introduce a more radically chord-based strategy into your approach to improvising on the blues. You are ready, in short, to begin playing the changes.

In the blues progression, the main harmonic movement over the first 8 bars is back and forth between the I-chord and the IV-chord. So far you have reflected this movement by going back and forth between the Major and Minor Blues Scales in the home key of the blues.

If you play the changes, however, what you will do is to move from the G Major Blues scale to the C Major Blues scale when the chords change. So the first 8 bars of a typical blues might look like this:

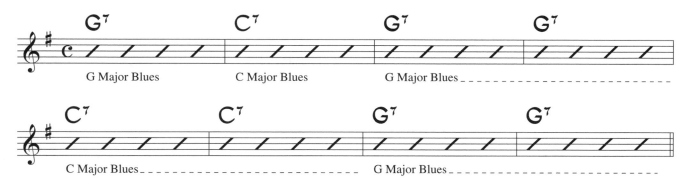

The following example of this approach (which we have simplified rhythmically to make it easier to read) comes from John Coltrane's improvised solo on the composition "Trane's Slo Blues," which you can hear on his classic album, "Lush Life."

As we see on the next page, Trane opens his solo with a phrase of descending 3rds, starting on the 5th degree of the G Major Blues Scale, with the 4th added.

In bar 2, when the chord changes to C7, Trane repeats the basic idea (descending 3rds starting on the 5th) using the C Major Blues Scale, with the 4th and the b7 added.

He then continues to use variations of this idea throughout his first chorus. If you keep your ears open you will hear innumerable examples of this approach in solos by the jazz masters.

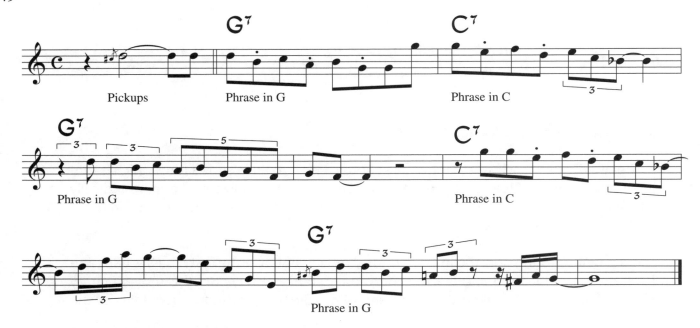

EXERCISE #27

Along with CD Track #5, try using this approach to playing on a blues, i.e., play phrases from the G Major Blues Scale on the G7 chords, the C Major Blues Scale on the C7 chords, and the D Major Blues Scale on the D7 chords.

EXERCISE #28

To end this chapter, please find **CD Track #13** which goes back and forth between two dominant 7th chords a whole step apart. Use the rhythm section accompaniment here to practice different variations of either Major or Minor Blues Scales on each chord.

Heading Towards Bebop

As you learn how to stretch the rules, you begin to get into making some real and consequential choices at every turn. The point of the process outlined in this book is to get you used to playing in a dynamic, shifting environment instead of a static one.

Once you get the hang of listening for and counting on the changes, you can start to deal with more complex changes and to entertain more options at the change points. And thus following the path we have laid out in this book will give you a firm foundation for further explorations into bebop and other jazz styles.

CHAPTER 4 • Applying The Blues Vocabulary

What we have practiced to this point is an approach to playing on major key blues progressions. But using the Blues Scales does not have to be limited only to the blues *per se*. Let's look at the possibilities of applying this blues-based improvisational strategy to other situations.

Modal Situations

First, jazz artists often use the Blues Scales as one of the choices they have when soloing on major, minor or dominant 7th chords, regardless of what happens in the rest of the song. Here is one example from Chick Corea's "Got A Match?" solo:

And here is an example from Michael Brecker, playing on "Bullet Train:"

In the next example, also from Michael Brecker, playing on Don Grolnick's tune "Pools," the harmony is basically modal, in E minor. But the chords do change briefly to the dominant of E minor (an altered B7 chord) before returning to E minor. Brecker stays with the E Minor Blues Scale throughout (adding the 9th at the beginning), rather than following the chords:

Here is one more modal example, near the beginning of John Coltrane's solo on "Resolution" from "A Love Supreme:"

"Bluesy" tunes

This category contains, on the major side, tunes such as "Doxy," "The Preacher" and "Groove Merchant," and, on the minor side, tunes such as "Work Song" and "Sugar." They all have a distinctively bluesy feel and their melodies make use of motifs that are derived from the Major and Minor Blues Scales. So, the blues vocabulary you have been building up will certainly come in handy here.

As you move away from the strictly blues forms, you need to pay closer attention to the written melody, as it will often give you hints as to how to to approach improvising on the song. Take, for example, Sonny Rollins' "Doxy," shown here:

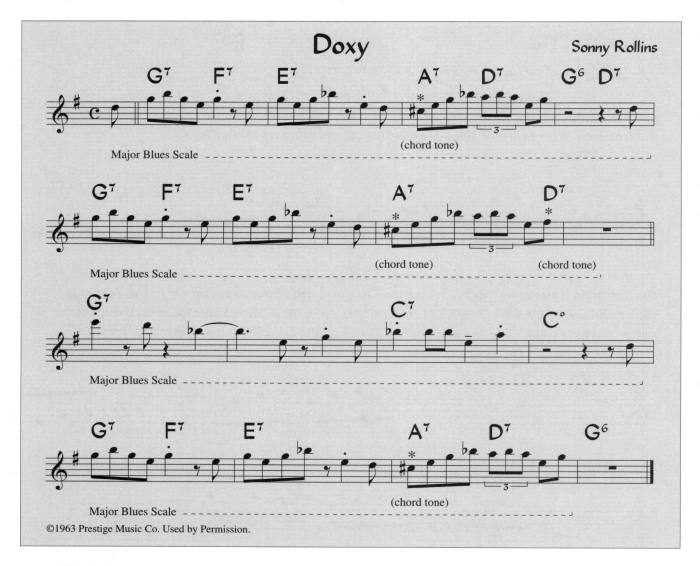

Doxy
Sonny Rollins

©1963 Prestige Music Co. Used by Permission.

EXERCISE #29

The melody of "Doxy" is derived primarily from the Major Blues Scale and so that scale should be your prime source of melodic material. On the II7 (A7) and V7 (D7) chords, however, the melody leaves the Major Blues Scale and so those bars would be a good time to use chord tones instead of staying strictly on the Major Blues Scale.

CD Track #14 will give you an accompaniment to work with on this classic jazz song.

Standards

Can the blues-based approach we have been studying be stretched or adapted to fit tunes such as the great "standards" from the 20th century American song tradition—tunes which rely heavily on ii7-V7-I and other common progressions? The answer is: on a limited basis, the blues vocabulary approach can indeed be adapted for these kinds of tunes.

One way you can use blues vocabulary is over any given ii7-V7-I chord progression, as in the following example from Clifford Brown, playing on the changes of "I'll Remember April." Brownie stays on the pure Minor Blues Scale through a four-bar ii7-V7-I progression.

The blues vocabulary may also be played over longer, more complex chord sequences, as in these two examples from Oscar Peterson, playing on "Just You, Just Me." He uses vocabulary from the Minor Blues Scale over a rapidly moving chord progression that includes a ii7-V7-I sequence. Note that Oscar sometimes adds the 6th to his Minor Blues Scale.

Jazz improvisers sometimes stick with blues vocabulary for much longer periods of time, playing through the chord progressions for entire sections of tunes. Here, for example, is Lester Young playing on "Almost Like Being In Love." He sticks with Major Blues Scale phrases through an entire 8-bar sequence.

Returning to Oscar Peterson's solo on "Just You, Just Me," we find another 8-bar sequence (an entire A section of the tune) in which he ignores the changes and stays with Minor Blues vocabulary:

And here is Stan Getz using the Minor Blues Scale for an extended period while playing on Bill Evans' minor key tune, "Funkallero:"

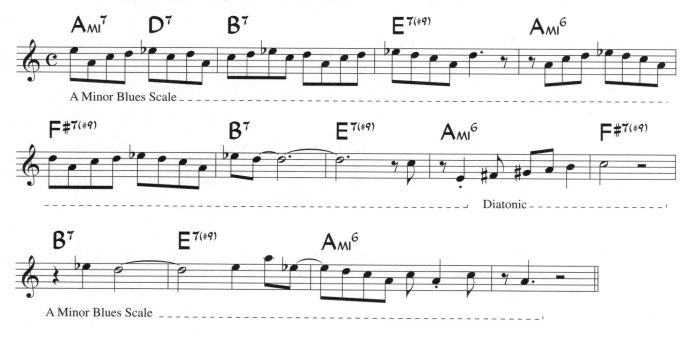

Finally, on the next page we include a 16-bar solo by Harry "Sweets" Edison, which he played on muted trumpet on a recording (with Billie Holiday) of the Gershwin standard, "They Can't Take That Away From Me." This one is especially interesting since "Sweets" plays the first 8 bars using vocabulary that is drawn exclusively drawn from the G Major Blues Scale, and then switches over to the G Minor Blues Scale for the next 8 bars before finally ending up in the Major mode.

Try this approach yourself by picking a typical major-key standard and playing phrases from one or both of the Blues Scales, instead of following the changes. On some tunes this will sound better than others, and it will require some experimentation to see what works. There are lots of play-along CDs that will help here, e.g., Jamey Aebersold's vast collection.

54

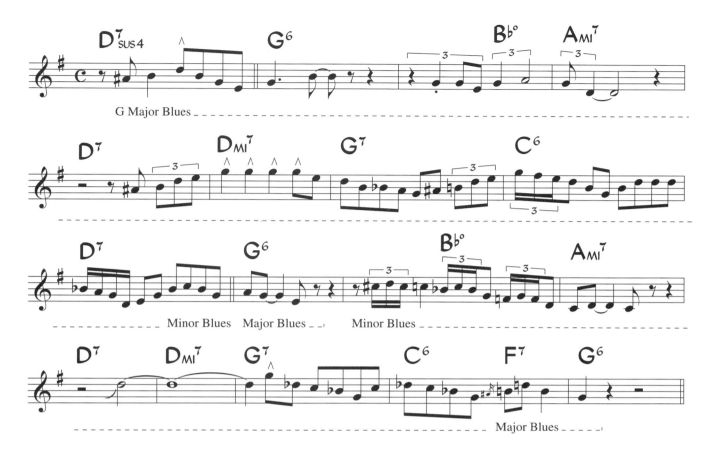

Photo©Paul Hoeffler, Toronto, ON

HARRY "SWEETS" EDISON
(with Buddy Tate)

55

Fusion

This same approach is also often used in the "fusion" style of improvising. David Sanborn, for example, in his solo on "Straight To The Heart," sometimes stays exclusively with a Minor Blues Scale for many bars at a time, regardless of the chord changes.

F# Minor Blues Scale

Elsewhere, Sanborn switches from the F# Minor Blues Scale to the A Minor Blues Scale at the point of a chord change:

F# Minor Blues Scale

A Minor Blues Scale

Sanborn will, occasionally, "stretch" his Minor Blues playing, as in this example where he uses the 2nd degree of the scale (E-natural) on "Hideaway."

D Minor Blues Scale

*
(add 2)

Final Exercises

EXERCISE #30

Finally, here is a sample solo on the changes of Duke Ellington's "In A Mellow Tone," incorporating many of the ideas we've presented in this book. Listen to the solo on **CD Track #15** then try playing it yourself . You can also use the CD Track without the saxophone channel as a play-along accompaniment to work on these same ideas.

EXERCISE #31

At the end of the CD you will find three tracks with simple blues progressions in A, E and C, so that you can practice what you have learned in the other most common keys in which jazz-style blues are played.

CD Track #16 Blues in A

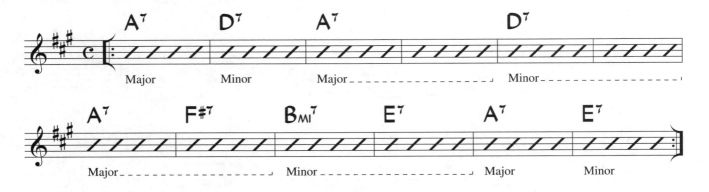

CD Track #17 Blues in E

CD Track #18 Blues in C

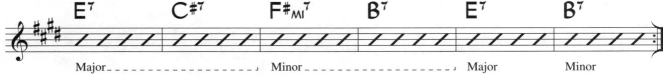

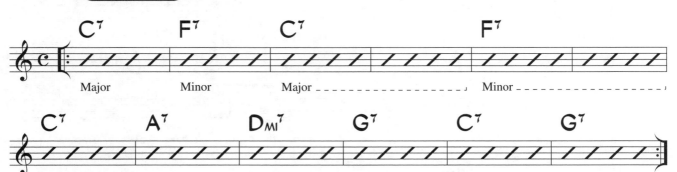

CD Track #19 consists of concert Bb and A tuning notes, for reference.

The Big Picture

The system we have presented here is actually fairly close to the approach taken by most of the early jazz improvisers during the 1920s and '30s, along with improvisers in more recent years whose style harkens back to that time. Such giants as Harry "Sweets" Edison, Ben Webster and Johnny Hodges all approached their improvised solos largely with a sophisticated blues vocabulary, a strong sense of tonality, and occasional reference to chords.

The blues vocabulary strategy lives on as a central device (although often in less pure form than with these earlier artists) in the playing of Swing Era musicians such as Paul Gonsalves, Illinois Jacquet and Jimmy Forrest; in artists associated with the "Soul" and "Funk" strains of jazz like Stanley Turrentine, Ramsey Lewis, Wes Montgomery, George Benson, Grover Washington, Maceo Parker and Dave Sanborn; in the "Texas Tenors" like Booker Ervin, Arnett Cobb, David "Fathead" Newman, and even, to an extent, Ornette Coleman.

For a huge proportion of other jazz artists, the blues-vocabulary strategy remains a viable option to be used, mixed in with other approaches. Charlie Parker, certainly, never discarded his blues vocabulary, even as he helped to create a new dialect—bebop. Cannonball Adderley employed a mix similar to Bird's, although with a greater proportion of blues phrases, especially in his later years. And contemporary artists such as Michael Brecker, John Scofield, Joshua Redman and James Carter all frequently revisit the vocabulary of the blues at times.

Overall, using blues vocabulary, especially in its expanded form as demonstrated in this book, represents a basic and very important approach to jazz improvisation. *When we hear a jazz player who never employs the blues-vocabulary strategy, who never abandons the chord-scale-interval approach that grew out of the bebop revolution, we often feel that something important is missing.*

For a number of improvising musicians, the blues vocabulary approach can be an end in itself. If you want to learn how to improvise on blues and bluesy tunes, or to play in swing bands, the blues vocabulary method presented in this book can give you most of what you need. In addition, improvisations in musical styles such as rock, rhythm and blues, and funk rarely sound authentic, and rarely connect with the listening and dancing audience, if they are not rooted in blues vocabulary.

We hope you have benefitted from this book and get many years of pleasure and musical growth returning to it!

Appendix A • Advanced Examples for Chapter 1

NOTE TO BEGINNERS: The information in the appendices will, no doubt, be beyond your current level of development. But one day, when you come back to this book again, you'll find a whole new treasure chest of ideas here.

Major and Minor Blues Scales in "Real Life"

You need to remember that the "rules" for blues improvising that we have given you really aren't rules at all. They are guidelines that are intended to help you organize your improvisations, to give them shape and movement.

Master improvisers generally do not improvise according to rules. Instead they hear different sounds and they try to relate those sounds to the chords in such a way as to make beautiful, swinging melodies that include plenty of contrast and variety. Moreover, they have developed many approaches other than the "Blues Scale" method to improvising on the blues, and they do not limit themselves to a single approach.

There are, however, a number of artists who come close enough to following the "rules" that they provide fairly clear illustrations of the system we've laid out so far, with the common exception that they might change scales a bit earlier or later than the "rules" would predict.

Here are a couple of Charlie Parker phrases that illustrate this point—the first from "K.C. Blues" and the second from "Visa:"

a)

b)

In sections of his solo on Herbie Hancock's "Watermelon Man" (transcribed on the next page), saxophonist Dexter Gordon comes pretty close to following the "rule" of using vocabulary derived from the Major Blues Scale on the I-chord (D7 in this case) and using ideas derived from the Minor Blues Scale on the other chords.

For example, his second chorus goes like this (please note that this is not a standard 12-bar blues form):

In the fourth chorus of his solo, he also alternates between the two scales, this time following a pattern which relates even more clearly to our guidelines:

Finally, here is another example of these guidelines at work (with a few more exceptions), this time from Eddie "Cleanhead" Vinson's saxophone solo on "Kidney Stew Blues:"

This excerpt originally appeared in "Jazz Styles And Analysis: Alto Sax" by Harry Miedema (Down Beat Music Workshop Publications.)

Photo©Chuck Stewart

EDDIE "CLEANHEAD" VINSON

Appendix B • Advanced Examples for Chapter 3

"Stretched" Blues Improvising in "Real Life"

Once we allow for the stretching of both the Blues Scales themselves (by the addition of notes) and the rules for using them (turning the rules into guidelines and allowing for exceptions), we begin to find a great many more instances of their use in actual jazz solos.

There are times when the switching between scales corresponds pretty closely to the Blues chord changes. Consider this example, the first seven bars of the second chorus of a Stanley Turrentine solo on a medium tempo blues, "Cherry Point:"

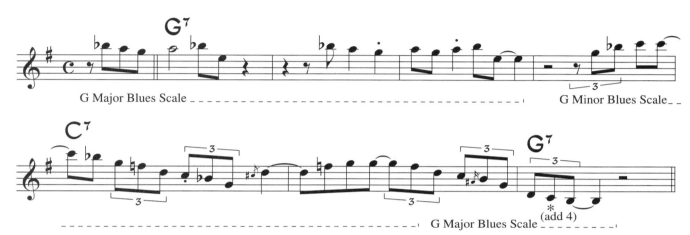

In the above passage, Stanley's improvisation actually follows quite closely the basic improvising rules you have learned in this book. At the beginning of the next chorus, however, he uses both scales, but not following our guidelines in terms of when he switches.

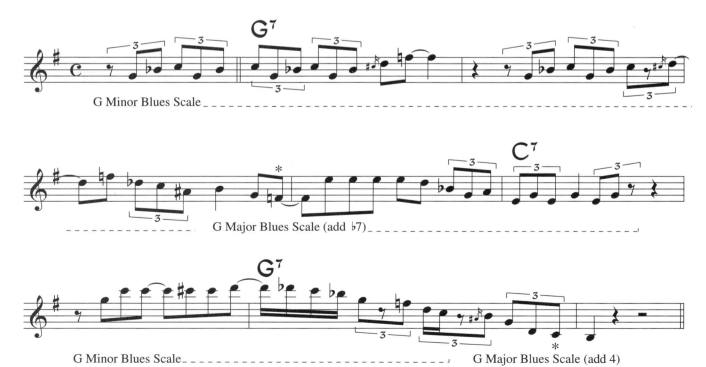

Turrentine has another interesting and unexpected switch at the end of his last chorus of this solo. We pick up the solo in bar 9 of the final chorus:

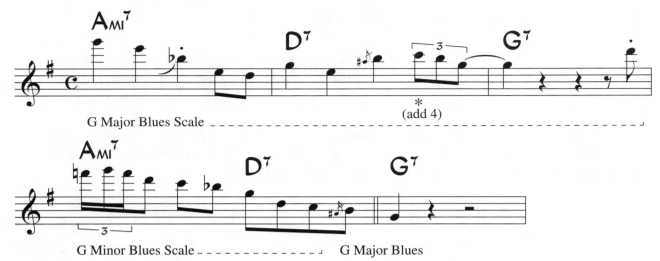

Here he draws his ideas from the Major Blues Scale (stretched to include the 4th) for the Ami7-D7 progression in bars 9 and 10 of the blues form. But when that progression repeats for the turnaround in bar 12, he uses the Minor Blues Scale, only to revert back to Major at the very last moment.

Again there is clear movement between Major and Minor, but the movement is determined by Turrentine's ear and overall compositional sense, rather than by a simple rigid rule.

Charlie Parker sometimes used an approach not unlike Turrentine's. For example, in his solo on "Now's The Time," Bird's second chorus begins with this:

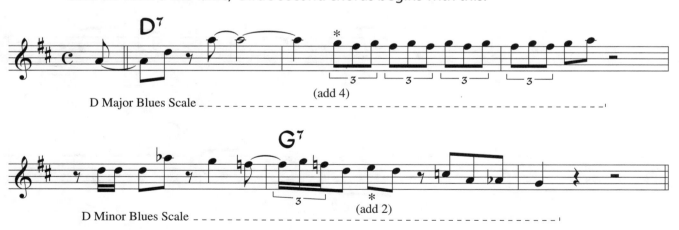

The work of other artists shows a great deal of freedom, stretching both the scales and the rules for movement between them. Here is a passage from the second chorus of Lee Morgan's famous solo on "The Sidewinder:"

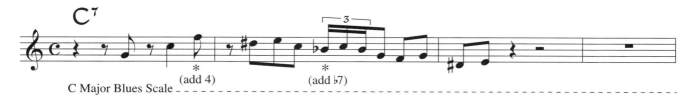

He stays, as the "rule" would suggest, in the Major Blues Scale on the C7 (I-chord), but he stretches the scale to include both the 4th and the b7th.

Cannonball Adderley's improvising vocabulary is rich with material derived from the Blues Scales. However, his Major Blues ideas are rarely "pure," either in the scale used or in the guidelines he follows for their use. Here are several examples from a couple of his better-known blues solos. First, from the beginning of the second chorus of Coltrane's blues, "The Sleeper:"

Our ears tell us that the above is a Major Blues idea used on the I-chord, but Cannonball's Major Blues scale includes the b7th, the 4th, and a chromatic note. Later, in the middle of the third chorus, we find this:

The idea above is a classic Major Blues lick with the b7th added. But notice that rather than relating to the tonality of the tune (C), it relates to the chord (F7). And Cannon also includes a very colorful #11 (B natural) in his phrase. So he has stretched both the scale and the rule.

Finally, from the same solo, at the end of the fourth chorus:

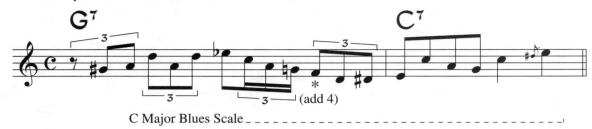

C Major Blues Scale

The whole idea above is derived from the Major Blues Scale (stretched to add the 4th), where our "rule" would lead us to expect the use of the Minor Blues Scale on the G7 (V-chord).

Cannonball's solo on Mile Davis' "Freddie The Freeloader" shows similar tendencies. At the top of the third chorus he plays this:

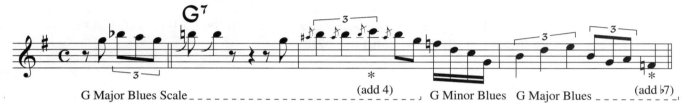

G Major Blues Scale   (add 4)   G Minor Blues   G Major Blues   (add ♭7)

The basic rule of the Major Blues scale on the G7 (I-chord) is followed, but he stretches the rule by inserting one brief Minor Blues idea into the middle of the longer Major Blues phrase. And he stretches the Major Blues scale itself by adding the by-now-familiar b7th and 4th. Later, in the next chorus, he uses this memorable idea:

C Major Blues Scale   (add ♭7)

Here he stretches both the rule and the scale, using a Major Blues idea derived from the chord (C) instead of the key (G), and adding the b7th to the scale at the end of the phrase.

Extended Use of the Major Blues Scale

Many artists will simply stay with one scale rather than switching back and forth. A very good example of this approach can be found in Miles Davis' solo on "Straight, No Chaser" from his 1958 Newport Jazz Festival recording. Consider his first chorus:

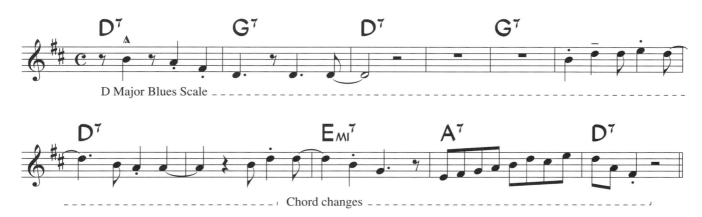

Here Miles sticks with the Major Blues scale vocabulary when the chord switches from I to IV, and never dips into his Minor Blues vocabulary. When he reaches the end of the chorus, he plays the chord changes in a diatonic fashion (using the D major scale), rather than moving to the Minor Blues vocabulary. His strategy is similar in the third chorus of the solo. Here, with pick-ups, are the first seven bars:

This is, again, strictly Major Blues. Elsewhere in the solo, Miles even uses Major Blues phrases on the ii7-V7-I chord sequence. Here are bars 8-11 of the sixth chorus:

Lest you begin to think that Miles never switches to Minor Blues licks, check out the fourth chorus of his solo, with pickups:

As you can see above, he switches from Major Blues to Minor Blues, and then ends the chorus by playing the chord changes in diatonic fashion. Miles employs a similar strategy at the beginning of the eighth and final chorus of the solo. Here are the first 7 bars, with pickups:

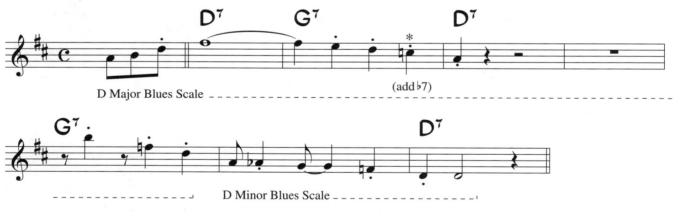

Miles Davis is by no means the only artist to stay with his Major Blues vocabulary even when the chord changes. Paul Desmond's solo on "The Blight Of The Stumble Bee" contains many examples of extended Major Blues improvisation. At the top of the next page is the final chorus of that solo:

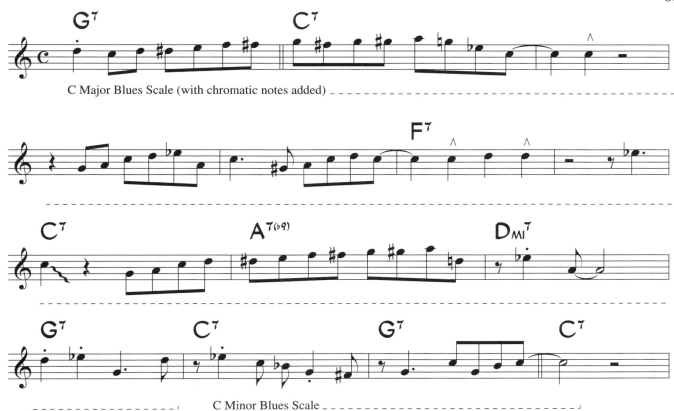

Desmond basically stays with a chromaticized version of the Major Blues scale throughout the chorus, only changing to the minor mode at the end, on the resolving C7 (I-chord) where, ironically, our guidelines tell us to expect the Major Blues scale.

Next is a good example of a composition that makes extensive use of the Major Blues Scale. But, instead of staying with a single scale in the home key of the piece, the composer (Jaco Pastorius), changes scales when the chords change, using the Major Blues Scale associated with the root of each chord. What follows are bars 3 through 7 of his song "Teen Town:"

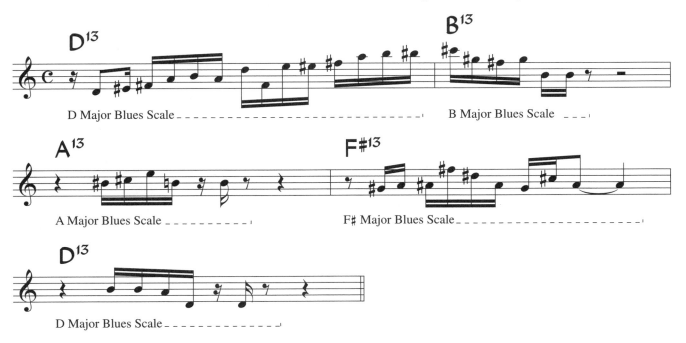

Extended use of the Minor Blues Scale

Perhaps even more common than extended use of the Major Blues Scale (even when the chords change) is extended use of the Minor Blues Scale. In the following example, an uptempo blues, Dexter Gordon creates an entire chorus out of a riff-like Minor Blues figure:

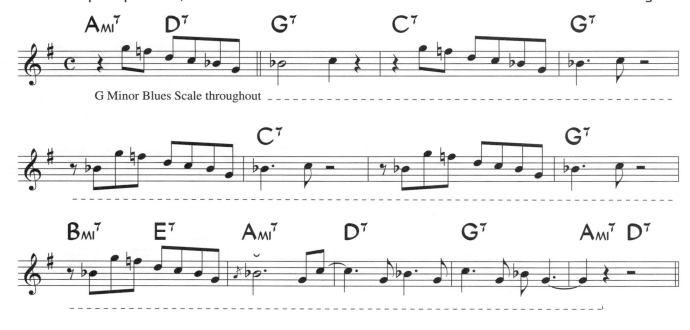

Stanley Turrentine is another artist who makes extensive use of the Minor Blues Scale: Here Turrentine reverses our basic guideline, using the Minor Blues Scale for the I-chord and the Major on the V-chord. What is instructive is that he does change the mode rather than sticking with either one for too long. (This passage may be played an octave above.)

The above excerpt originally appeared in "Masters Of The Tenor Saxophone Play The Blues: Jazz Tenor Solos" by Trent Kynaston, (Corybant Productions, 1988).

Here are some examples of extended Minor Blues Scale improvisation by Dizzy Gillespie, playing on Duke Ellington's "The Mooche." We start this first passage in bar 5 of a 12-bar blues chorus:

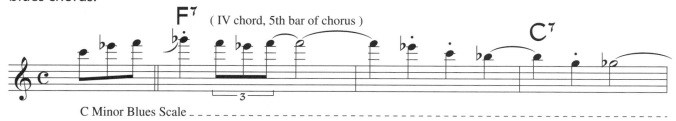

We get an even more extended minor mode interpretation in a later chorus, again picking up in bar 5 after an ensemble "shout" section:

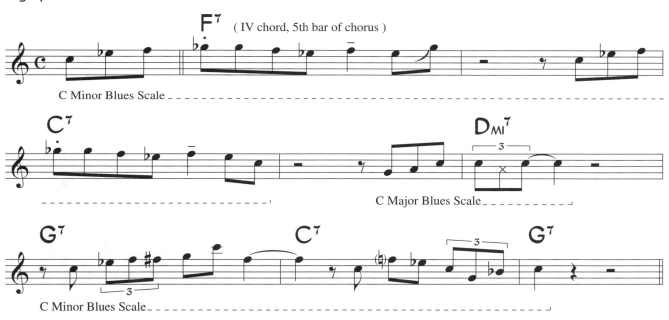

Later in the same solo, we hear him use the Minor Blues Scale on the I-chord (C7) at the top of a chorus. Only Dizzy's pickup note is outside of the pure Minor Blues Scale in this luscious phrase.

Understanding Extended Use of the Minor Blues Scale

One of the most important points of this book is to open your eyes to the world of the Major Blues scale and its variants. In so doing, we are trying to push you away from the prevailing method of basic jazz instruction, which would have you rely exclusively on what we have termed the "Minor Blues Scale."

However, there are, as we have clearly seen from the examples included above, times when reliance on Minor Blues vocabulary is musically valid. So, you should by no means rule out extended use of the minor mode. What you need is an understanding of its context in your overall development as an improviser.

If you start out thinking that the basic structural principle of improvising on the blues is simply the Minor Blues Scale, you will run into the problems we discussed in Chapter 1. Your solos on the blues will, in all likelihood, suffer from the relentless contradiction between the minor mode of your improvising scale and the major sound of the tune's harmony. But if you see the basic structural principle as including both the Major and Minor Blues Scales, and that there must be movement between the two—and that eventually you will "stretch" both the scales and the rules for movement between the two—you have a foundation that will enable you to play interesting, well-developed, harmonically satisfying solos.

In this context, extended use of the Minor Blues Scale becomes one possible musical strategy for "stretching" the blues, rather than the only strategy available to you. Dizzy, Dexter, Stanley, and the rest of the great jazz artists, did not play extended Minor Blues Scale phrases because it was the only thing they knew how to do. They played it because it gave them the musical sound and mood that they were looking for at that point in time.

Photo©Chuck Stewart   **STANLEY TURRENTINE**

Appendix C • Advanced Examples for Chapter 4

Blues Scales in Non-Blues Improvising

Here are some more advanced examples of the idea of using blues vocabulary on non-blues songs. Here we see Freddie Hubbard playing the following on his second chorus of "Up Jumped Spring." The tune is in no way a blues, but Freddie's ideas here sound very "blue" indeed.

Next we look at part of a Zoot Sims' solo on "Mack The Knife," harkening back to Lester Young's style. Like Freddie, Zoot uses both scales. Note that he saves the Minor Blues Scale for the dominant chord (D7) as a way of getting back to the tonic.

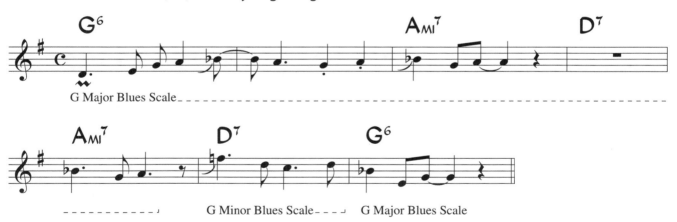

Blues Scales in Non-Blues Compositions

Many of the composers of jazz tunes use the Major and Minor Blues Scales even when their compositions do not relate directly to established blues form. A good example of this is Jerome Richardson's "Groove Merchant."

The approach here is somewhat different than "Doxy" in that Richardson makes almost no reference whatever to the chords. He sticks exclusively with the Major Blues Scale through the first 12 bars, stretching the scale only to add chromatic passing tones. Finally in bar 13 he adds a chord tone. Then in bar 15, on the final resolving part of the chord progression, he switches to the Minor Blues Scale to bring the tune home.

Another tune which uses phrases taken from both the Major and Minor Blues Scales is Horace Silver's "Sister Sadie." This is a 32-bar tune, with the first 8 bars repeating as the last 8 after the bridge.

The entire song is derived from the E Blues scales, with the first 7 bars of the A section being pure Major Blues, and the last bar being pure Minor Blues. The bridge is entirely built on the Minor Blues Scale, stretched to include the 2nd degree of the scale.

Another Horace Silver tune, "Juicy Lucy," uses only Major Blues Scale phrases, but they are transposed to the important key centers of the song, which is based on Charlie Parker's "Confirmation."

In the first four bars of the 'A' section, Horace repeats an D Major Blues Scale phrase, while the chords change underneath the phrase. At each modulation, Horace introduces a new Major Blues phrase based on the new key. Play through the tune and see how this works for yourself.

More Blues Scales in Non-Blues Improvising

The tradition of using Blues vocabulary in non-blues situations has a long and rich history. Consider, for example, how Buster Smith—an important figure because of his influence on Charlie Parker—handles the I-chord on "Moten Swing." Three examples follow:

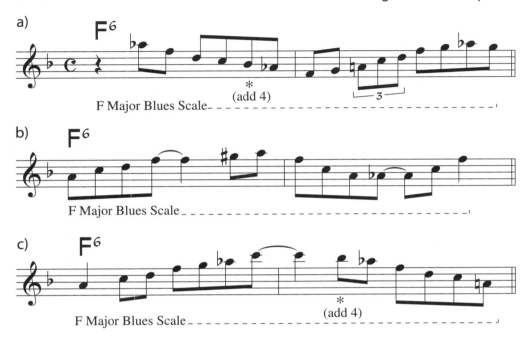

Johnny Hodges was another proponent of the sound of the Major Blues vocabulary. The following example is from a tune called "Whoa Babe," which uses "I Got Rhythm" changes:

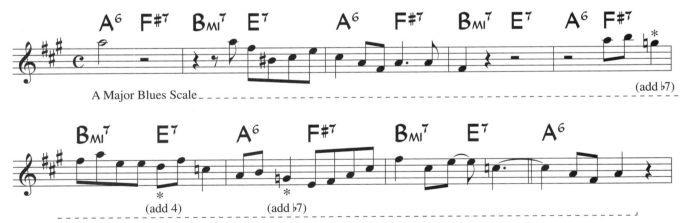

The above two excerpts originally appeared in "Jazz Styles And Analysis: Alto Sax" by Harry Miedema (Down Beat Music Workshop Publications).

77

A more sophisticated and interesting example can be found in the work of alto player Art Pepper. This is the first 16 bars of his solo on the standard "Broadway," including the pickups. Notice how he moves smoothly back and forth between Major Blues and Minor Blues vocabulary, making the changes as his ear dictates.

This excerpt originally appeared in "Jazz Styles And Analysis: Alto Sax" by Harry Miedema (Down Beat Music Workshop Publications).

Here are some other, shorter examples of the use of Blues Scales in improvising on tunes that are not in any way definable as "blues."

The first is from Hank Mobley's solo on his tune "This I Dig Of You." For the first half of this eight-bar passage, Mobley abandons the chord changes and sticks with the Minor Blues Scale in the home key of G. Then for the last 4 bars, he follows the chord changes closely.

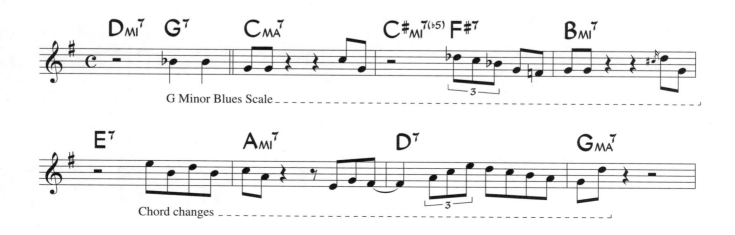

Next is a beautiful excerpt from Michel Petrucciani soloing on the ballad "A Portrait Of Jennie."

Finally, here is a more extended use of Blues Scales on "I Got Rhythm" changes. The artist is tenor saxophonist Bob Berg, and the passage below includes the last 8 bars of the second chorus and the first 14 bars of the third chorus of his solo on "Steppin:"

The above excerpt originally appeared in "Masters Of The Tenor Saxophone: Bob Berg Jazz Tenor Solos" by Trent Kynaston, (Corybant Productions, 1987).

Blues Song List

Following is a list of blues tunes to be found in various Sher Music Co. fake books. But please don't rely just on the sheet music—find and listen to the masters of jazz play these tunes so that you can hear what is possible to express without leaving the roots of jazz behind.

NRB1 = The New Real Book - Volume 1
NRB2 = The New Real Book - Volume 2
NRB3 = The New Real Book - Volume 3
AJRB = The All Jazz Real Book
REB1 = The Real Easy Book - Volume 1
REB2 = The Real Easy Book - Volume 2
WGFB = The World's Greatest Fake Book
SRB = The Standards Real Book
LRB = The Latin Real Book.

All these books are available from Sher Music Co. at www.shermusic.com or at most retail music stores world-wide.

Song	As Played By	Book
1. 2 Degrees East, 3 Degrees West	John Lewis	AJRB
2. Azure-Té	Standard	REB2
3. Bags' Groove	Milt Jackson	REB1, SRB
4. Bass Blues	John Coltrane	NRB2
5. Bessie's Blues	John Coltrane	NRB2
6. Blue Seven	Sonny Rollins	AJRB, REB1
7. Blues By Five	Miles Davis	REB1
8. Blues For Alice	Charlie Parker	NRB2
9. Blues In The Closet	Oscar Pettiford	REB1
10. Blues March	Benny Golsen	REB2
11. Blues On The Corner	McCoy Tyner	NRB1
12. Byrd Like	Freddie Hubbard	REB2
13. Cedar's Blues	Cedar Walton	REB2
14. Chitlins Con Carne	Kenny Burrell	AJRB, REB2
15. Cousin Mary	John Coltrane	REB2
16. Don't Get Scared	King Pleasure	REB2
17. Doodlin'	Horace Silver	SRB
18. The Double Up	Lee Morgan	NRB3
19. Down	Miles Davis	AJRB
20. Eighty One	Miles Davis	NRB1
21. Equinox	John Coltrane	NRB2, REB1
22. Filthy McNasty	Horace Silver	NRB2
23. Footprints	Wayne Shorter	NRB1
24. Freight Trane	Tommy Flanagan	WGFB
25. In A Hurry	Christian McBride	AJRB

Song	As Played By	Book
26. Mamacita	Joe Henderson	NRB3
27. Mamblues	Cal Tjader	LRB
28. Mambo Influenciado	Chucho Valdez	LRB
29. Mr. Day	John Coltrane	REB2
30. Mr. P.C.	John Coltrane	AJRB, REB1
31. On The Marc	Eric Alexander	REB2
32. One For Daddy-O	Miles Davis	REB1
33. Opus De Funk	Horace Silver	NRB3
34. Rakin' And Scrapin'	Harold Mabern	REB2
35. Red's Good Groove	Red Garland	REB1
36. Revelation	Kenny Barron	REB1
37. Sack Of Woe	Cannonball Adderley	REB2
38. Sandu	Clifford Brown	NRB1
39. Scotch And Water	Cannonball Adderley	REB2
40. Senor Blues	Horace Silver	NRB2
41. Sir John	Blue Mitchell	REB1
42. Some Other Blues	John Coltrane	NRB2, REB2
43. Sonnymoon For Two	Sonny Rollins	REB1
44. Swinging Til The Girls Come Home	Lambert, Hendricks & Ross	AJRB
45. Tee Pee Time	Clark Terry	REB2
46. Tenor Madness	Sonny Rollins	REB1
47. Twisted	Annie Ross	NRB1
48. Walkin'	Miles Davis	SRB, REB2
49. West Coast Blues	Wes Montgomery	NRB1, REB2
50. When Will The Blues Leave	Ornette Coleman	AJRB

Latin Music Books & CDs from Sher Music Co.

The Latin Real Book (C, Bb or Eb)

The only professional-level Latin fake book ever published! Over 570 pages. Includes detailed transcriptions of tunes, exactly as recorded by:

Ray Barretto	Irakere	Andy Narell	Ft. Apache Band	Djavan
Eddie Palmieri	Celia Cruz	Mario Bauza	Dave Valentin	Tom Jobim
Fania All-Stars	Arsenio Rodriguez	Dizzy Gilllespie	Paquito D'Rivera	Toninho Horta
Tito Puente	Tito Rodriguez	Mongo Santamaria	Clare Fischer	Joao Bosco
Ruben Blades	Orquesta Aragon	Manny Oquendo & Libre	Chick Corea	Milton Nascimento
Los Van Van	Beny Moré	Puerto Rico All-Stars	Sergio Mendes	Leila Pinheiro
NG La Banda	Cal Tjader	Issac Delgaldo	Ivan Lins	Gal Costa
				And Many More!

Muy Caliente!

Afro-Cuban Play-Along CD and Book
Rebeca Mauleón - Keyboard
Oscar Stagnaro - Bass
Orestes Vilató - Timbales
Carlos Caro - Bongos
Edgardo Cambon - Congas
Over 70 min. of smokin' Latin grooves! Stereo separation so you can eliminate the bass or piano. Play-along with a rhythm section featuring some of the top Afro-Cuban musicians in the world!

The Latin Real Book Sampler CD

12 of the greatest Latin Real Book tunes as played by the original artists: Tito Puente, Ray Barretto, Andy Narell, Puerto Rico Allstars, Bacacoto, etc. $16 list price. Available in U.S.A. only.

101 Montunos

by Rebeca Mauleón
The only comprehensive study of Latin piano playing ever published.
• Bi-lingual text (English/Spanish)
• 2 CDs of the author demonstrating each montuno
• Covers over 100 years of Afro-Cuban styles, including the danzón, guaracha, mambo, merengue and songo—from Peruchin to Eddie Palmieri.

The True Cuban Bass

By Carlos Del Puerto, (bassist with Irakere) and **Silvio Vergara**, $22.

For acoustic or electric bass; English and Spanish text; Includes CDs of either historic Cuban recordings or Carlos playing each exercise; Many transcriptions of complete bass parts for tunes in different Cuban styles – the roots of Salsa.

The Brazilian Guitar Book

by Nelson Faria, one of Brazil's best new guitarists.
• Over 140 pages of comping patterns, transcriptions and chord melodies for samba, bossa, baiaõ, etc.
• Complete chord voicings written out for each example.
• Comes with a CD of Nelson playing each example.
• The most complete Brazilian guitar method ever published! $28 list price.

Joe Diorio – "Nelson Faria's book is a welcome addition to the guitar literature. I'm sure those who work with this volume wiill benefit greatly"

The Salsa Guide Book

By Rebeca Mauleón
The only complete method book on salsa ever published! 260 pages. $25

Carlos Santana – "A true treasure of knowledge and information about Afro-Cuban music."
Mark Levine, author of The *Jazz Piano Book*. – "This is the book on salsa."
Sonny Bravo, pianist with Tito Puente – "This will be the salsa 'bible' for years to come."
Oscar Hernández, pianist with Rubén Blades – "An excellent and much needed resource."

The New Real Book Series

The Standards Real Book (C, Bb or Eb)

Alice In Wonderland
All Of You
Alone Together
At Last
Baltimore Oriole
A Beautiful Friendship
Bess, You Is My Woman
But Not For Me
Close Enough For Love
Crazy He Calls Me
Dancing In The Dark
Days Of Wine And Roses
Dreamsville
Easy To Love
Embraceable You

Falling In Love With Love
From This Moment On
Give Me The Simple Life
Have You Met Miss Jones?
Hey There
I Can't Get Started
I Concentrate On You
I Cover The Waterfront
I Love You
I Loves You Porgy
I Only Have Eyes For You
I Wish I Knew
I'm A Fool To Want You
Indian Summer

It Ain't Necessarily So
It Never Entered My Mind
It's You Or No One
Just One Of Those Things
Love For Sale
Love Walked In
Lover, Come Back To Me
The Man I Love
Mr. Lucky
My Funny Valentine
My Heart Stood Still
My Man's Gone Now
Old Folks
On A Clear Day

Our Love Is Here To Stay
Secret Love
September In The Rain
Serenade In Blue
Shiny Stockings
Since I Fell For You
So In Love
So Nice (Summer Samba)
Some Other Time
Stormy Weather
The Summer Knows
Summer Night
Summertime
Teach Me Tonight

That Sunday, That Summer
Then I'll Be Tired Of You
There's No You
A Time For Love
Time On My Hands
'Tis Autumn
Where Or When
Who Cares?
With A Song In My Heart
You Go To My Head
Ain't No Sunshine
'Round Midnight
The Girl From Ipanema
Bluesette
And Hundreds More!

The New Real Book - Volume 1 (C, Bb or Eb)

Angel Eyes
Anthropology
Autumn Leaves
Beautiful Love
Bernie's Tune
Blue Bossa
Blue Daniel
But Beautiful
Chain Of Fools
Chelsea Bridge
Compared To What
Darn That Dream
Desafinado
Early Autumn
Eighty One

E.S.P.
Everything Happens To Me
Fall
Feel Like Makin' Love
Footprints
Four
Four On Six
Gee Baby Ain't I Good To
You
Gone With The Wind
Here's That Rainy Day
I Love Lucy
I Mean You
I Should Care
I Thought About You

If I Were A Bell
Imagination
The Island
Jersey Bounce
Joshua
Lady Bird
Like Someone In Love
Line For Lyons
Little Sunflower
Lush Life
Mercy, Mercy, Mercy
The Midnight Sun
Monk's Mood
Moonlight In Vermont
My Shining Hour

Nature Boy
Nefertiti
Nothing Personal
Oleo
Once I Loved
Out Of This World
Pent Up House
Polkadots And
Moonbeams
Portrait Of Tracy
Put It Where You Want It
Robbin's Nest
Ruby, My Dear
Satin Doll
Search For Peace

Shaker Song
Skylark
A Sleepin' Bee
Solar
Speak No Evil
St. Thomas
Street Life
Tenderly
These Foolish Things
This Masquerade
Three Views Of A Secret
Waltz For Debby
Willow Weep For Me
And Many More!

The New Real Book - Volume 2 (C, Bb or Eb)

Afro-Centric
After You've Gone
Along Came Betty
Bessie's Blues
Black Coffee
Blues For Alice
Body And Soul
Bolivia
The Boy Next Door
Bye Bye Blackbird
Cherokee
A Child Is Born
Cold Duck Time
Day By Day

Django
Equinox
Exactly Like You
Falling Grace
Five Hundred Miles High
Freedom Jazz Dance
Giant Steps
Got A Match?
Harlem Nocturne
Hi-Fly
Honeysuckle Rose
I Hadn't Anyone 'Til You
I'll Be Around
I'll Get By

Ill Wind
I'm Glad There Is You
Impressions
In Your Own Sweet Way
It's The Talk Of The Town
Jordu
Killer Joe
Lullaby Of The Leaves
Manha De Carneval
The Masquerade Is Over
Memories Of You
Moment's Notice
Mood Indigo
My Ship

Naima
Nica's Dream
Once In A While
Perdido
Rosetta
Sea Journey
Senor Blues
September Song
Seven Steps To Heaven
Silver's Serenade
So Many Stars
Some Other Blues
Song For My Father
Sophisticated Lady

Spain
Stablemates
Stardust
Sweet And Lovely
That's All
There Is No Greater Love
'Til There Was You
Time Remembered
Turn Out The Stars
Unforgettable
While We're Young
Whisper Not
Will You Still Be Mine?
You're Everything
And Many More!

The New Real Book - Volume 3 (C, Bb, Eb or Bass clef)

Actual Proof
Ain't That Peculiar
Almost Like Being In Love
Another Star
Autumn Serenade
Bird Of Beauty
Black Nile
Blue Moon
Butterfly
Caravan
Ceora
Close Your Eyes
Creepin'
Day Dream

Dolphin Dance
Don't Be That Way
Don't Blame Me
Emily
Everything I Have Is
Yours
For All We Know
Freedomland
The Gentle Rain
Get Ready
A Ghost Of A Chance
Heat Wave
How Sweet It Is
I Fall In Love Too Easily

I Got It Bad
I Hear A Rhapsody
If You Could See Me Now
In A Mellow Tone
In A Sentimental Mood
Inner Urge
Invitation
The Jitterbug Waltz
Just Friends
Just You, Just Me
Knock On Wood
The Lamp Is Low
Laura
Let's Stay Together
Litha

Lonely Woman
Maiden Voyage
Moon And Sand
Moonglow
My Girl
On Green Dolphin Street
Over The Rainbow
Prelude To A Kiss
Respect
Ruby
The Second Time Around
Serenata
The Shadow Of Your Smile
So Near, So Far
Solitude

Speak Like A Child
Spring Is Here
Stairway To The Stars
Star Eyes
Stars Fell On Alabama
Stompin' At The Savoy
Sugar
Sweet Lorraine
Taking A Chance On Love
This Is New
Too High
(Used To Be A) Cha Cha
When Lights Are Low
You Must Believe In Spring
And Many More!

Other Jazz Publications

The Jazz Theory Book

By Mark Levine, the most comprehensive Jazz Theory book ever published! $38 list price.
- Over 500 pages of text and over 750 musical examples.
- Written in the language of the working jazz musician, this book is easy to read and user-friendly. At the same time, it is the most comprehensive study of jazz harmony and theory ever published.
- Mark Levine has worked with Bobby Hutcherson, Cal Tjader, Joe Henderson, Woody Shaw, and many other jazz greats.

The Jazz Piano Book

By Mark Levine, Concord recording artist and pianist with Cal Tjader. For beginning to advanced pianists. The only truly comprehensive method ever published! Over 300 pages. $32

Richie Beirach – "The best new method book available."
Hal Galper – "This is a must!"
Jamey Aebersold – "This is an invaluable resource for any pianist."
James Williams – "One of the most complete anthologies on jazz piano."
Now available in Spanish too! ¡El Libro del Jazz Piano!

The Improvisor's Bass Method

By Chuck Sher. A complete method for electric or acoustic bass, plus transcribed solos and bass lines by Mingus, Jaco, Ron Carter, Scott LaFaro, Paul Jackson, Ray Brown, and more! Over 200 pages. $16

International Society of Bassists – "Undoubtedly the finest book of its kind."

Eddie Gomez – "Informative, readily comprehensible and highly imaginative"

Concepts For Bass Soloing

By Chuck Sher and Marc Johnson, (bassist with Bill Evans, etc.) The only book ever published that is specifically designed to improve your soloing! $26
- Includes two CDs of Marc Johnson soloing on each exercise
- Transcriptions of bass solos by: Eddie Gomez, John Patitucci, Scott LaFaro, Jimmy Haslip, etc.

"It's a pleasure to encounter a Bass Method so well conceived and executed." – **Steve Swallow**

The Yellowjackets Songbook

Complete package contains six separate spiral-bound books, one each for:
- Piano/partial score • C melody lead sheet
- Synthesizer/miscellaneous parts
- Bb & Eb Horn melody part • Bass • Drums

Contains 20 great tunes from their entire career. Charts exactly as recorded – approved by the Yellowjackets. World famous Sher Music Co. accuracy and legibility. Over 400 pages, $38 list price.

The Jazz Solos of Chick Corea

Over 150 pages of Chick's greatest solos; "Spain", "Litha", "Windows", "Sicily", etc. for all instrumentalists, single line transcriptions, not full piano score. $18

Chick Corea – "I don't know anyone I would trust more to correctly transcribe my improvisations."

The World's Greatest Fake Book

Jazz & Fusion Tunes by: **Coltrane, Mingus, Jaco, Chick Corea, Bird, Herbie Hancock, Bill Evans, McCoy, Beirach, Ornette, Wayne Shorter, Zawinul, AND MANY MORE!** $32

Chick Corea – "Great for any students of jazz.'
Dave Liebman – "The fake book of the 80's."
George Cables – "The most carefully conceived fake book I've ever seen."

African Percussion, The Djembe

The first comprehensive djembe method book ever published.
- CD included of the author, Serge Blanc, playing each section of the book.
- Includes 22 great standards of traditional djembe music.
- Duet and trios writtten out so you can start playing and practising in groups.

The New Real Book Play-Along CDs (For Volume 1)

CD #1 - Jazz Classics - Lady Bird, Bouncin' With Bud, Up Jumped Spring, Monk's Mood, Doors, Very Early, Eighty One, Voyage & More!
CD #2 - Choice Standards - Beautiful Love, Darn That Dream, Moonlight In Vermont, Trieste, My Shining Hour, I Should Care & More!
CD #3 - Pop-Fusion - Morning Dance, Nothing Personal, La Samba, Hideaway, This Masquerade, Three Views Of A Secret, Rio & More!
World-Class Rhythm Sections, featuring Mark Levine, Larry Dunlap, Sky Evergreen, Bob Magnusson, Keith Jones, Vince Lateano & Tom Hayashi

Recent Sher Music Publications

The Real Easy Book Vol. 1
TUNES FOR BEGINNING IMPROVISERS
Published by Sher Music Co. in conjunction with the Stanford Jazz Workshop. $19 list price.
The easiest tunes from Horace Silver, Eddie Harris, Freddie Hubbard, Red Garland, Sonny Rollins, Cedar Walton, Wes Montgomery Cannonball Adderly, etc.

Get yourself or your beginning jazz combo sounding good right away with the first fake book ever designed for the beginning improviser.
Available in C, Bb, Eb and Bass Clef.

The Real Easy Book Vol. 2
TUNES FOR INTERMEDIATE IMPROVISERS
Published by Sher Music Co. in conjunction with the Stanford Jazz Workshop. Over 240 pages.$29.
The best intermediate-level tunes by: Charlie Parker, John Coltrane, Miles Davis, John Scofield, Sonny Rollins, Horace Silver, Wes Montgomery, Freddie Hubbard, Cal Tjader, Cannonball Adderly, and more!

Both volumes feature instructional material tailored for each tune. Perfect for jazz combos!
Available in C, Bb, Eb and Bass Clef.

The All Jazz Real Book
Over 540 pages of tunes as recorded by: Miles, Trane, Bill Evans, Cannonball, Scofield, Brecker, Yellowjackets, Bird, Mulgrew Miller, Kenny Werner, MJQ, McCoy Tyner, Kurt Elling, Brad Mehldau, Don Grolnick, Kenny Garrett, Patitucci, Jerry Bergonzi, Stanley Clarke, Tom Harrell, Herbie Hancock, Horace Silver, Stan Getz, Sonny Rollins, and MORE!
Includes a free CD of many of the melodies (featuring Bob Sheppard & Friends.). $44 list price.
Available in C, Bb, Eb

The Latin Bass Book
A PRACTICAL GUIDE
By Oscar Stagnaro
The only comprehensive book ever published on how to play bass in authentic Afro-Cuban, Brazilian, Caribbean, Latin Jazz & South American styles.
$34 list price
Over 250 pages of transcriptions of Oscar Stagnaro playing each exercise. Learn from the best!

Includes: 3 Play-Along CDs to accompany each exercise, featuring world-class rhythm sections.

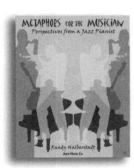

Metaphors For The Musician
By Randy Halberstadt
This practical and enlightening book will help any jazz player or vocalist look at music with "new eyes." Designed for any level of player, on any instrument, "Metaphors For The Musician" provides numerous exercises throughout to help the reader turn these concepts into musical reality.
Guaranteed to help you improve your musicianship.
330 pages - $29 list price. Satisfaction guaranteed!

Inside The Brazilian Rhythm Section
By Nelson Faria and Cliff Korman
This is the first book/CD package ever published that provides an opportunity for bassists, guitarists, pianists and drummers to interact and play-along with a master Brazilian rhythm section. Perfect for practicing both accompanying and soloing.
$28 list price for book and 2 CDs - including the charts for the CD tracks and sample parts for each instrument, transcribed from the recording.. Satisfaction guaranteed!

The finest in Jazz & Latin publications
SHER MUSIC CO.
www.shermusic.com